The Official
Little Smitty Joke Book

By

Tim "Smitty" Smith

Illustrated By Randy Gray II

www.jokewithsmitty.com

Published by Tim "Smitty" Smith

ISBN 979-8-9884227-0-9

Library of Congress Number: 2023910129

Wet Dreams

A wealthy man was looking over the ocean when he said to himself, "I think I am going to buy an Oceanliner!" Little Smitty overheard the man. He replied, "You should have spread that out before they put the water in!"

Colored Greens

Little Smitty was in a restaurant when he overheard a man ask the waitress, "Do y'all serve collards here?" Little Smitty spoke up and said, "Yes sir. They serve EVERYBODY here!"

Bob and Edith Caking It Up

Little Smitty: "Edith owned a bakery. Bob went in for the first time and bought a cake. He saw her and instantly fell for her! Every week he went back and bought a cake whether he ate it or not! After two years of dating, they got married! What do you think of that?" Friend: "I don't know Little Smitty! What do YOU think?" Little Smitty: "I guess Bob can have his cake and Edith too!"

Smitty At School

Teacher: "Little Smitty, can you use the word "Waikiki" in a sentence?"

Little Smitty: "Why I sure can. My sister asked KeKe's mom if she could go on an all-girls trip with her. Her mom said, "No!" My persistent sister asked her, Waikiki can't go with me?"

Teacher: "Little Smitty, can you use the word "arachnophobias" in a sentence?"

Little Smitty: "Why I think I can handle that one. One time, I took a spider out for drinks. The bartender gave me and the "arachnophobias" on the house!"

Teacher: "Little Smitty, can you use the word "Pikachu" in two separate sentences?" Little Smitty: "Yup yup! A Peeping Tom's purpose is to take a "Pikachu" through your window. Second sentence - My friend couldn't choose what brand of chewing tobacco he wanted. So after 15 minutes, I said, "Come on man. Just "Pikachu" and let's get the hell out of here!"

Teacher: "Little Smitty, can you use the word "intense" in a sentence?"
Little Smitty: "I sure can. That group of people over there camping are intense!"

Teacher: Little Smitty, can you use the word "comet" in a sentence?"
Little Smitty: "Sure teach! I used to clean my tub with Comet. But then he got mad and told Blitzen that he didn't want to be a scrub brush anymore!"

Teacher: "Little Smitty, can you spell?"
Little Smitty: "Hell yeah! HOCUS POCUS!"

Teacher: "Little Smitty, what is one good lesson that we can learn from cows?"
Little Smitty: "Do unto udders as they do to us?" Teacher: "GET OUT!"

Teacher: "Little Smitty, can you use the word "acetaminophen" in a sentence?" Little Smitty: "Duh, yeah! Anyway, me and my friend went to a pond to catch some minnows. I said, "Did you know that minnows have fins?" My friend replied, "Of course, 'acetaminophen" on this one I caught!"

Teacher: "Little Smitty, what would a butcher say to a potential blind date?" Little Smitty: "I'd really love to meat with you!"

Teacher: "So today, class we are going to learn about Paul Bunyon!" Little Smitty: "Excuse me teach, but why are we learning about a man's foot problems?"

Teacher: "Little Smitty, can you use the word "thespian" in a sentence?" Little Smitty: "Oh hecky yeah! My neighbor made everybody at his pool party leave.

He told them, "I want EVERYBODY out cause "thespian" in my pool!"

Teacher: "Little Smitty, What are the numbers 1,3,5,7,9 and 11 called? Little Smitty: "I don't EVEN know!"

Teacher: "Little Smitty, what is something you should never say to someone who works at a sperm bank?" Little Smitty: "You've got to be kidding!"

Teacher: "Little Smitty, can you use the phrase common sense in a sentence?" Little Smitty: "Sure can. Two or more people that stink usually have common scents!"

Teacher: "Little Smitty, do you know what the meaning of protocol is?" Little Smitty: "I sure do. It's when an NFL player has a bad toe and calls the foot doctor! Pro toe call."

Teacher: "Little Smitty, can you tell me the definition of the algorithm?" Little Smitty: "Aww yeah! That's an easy one. It's when Al Gore is dancing pretty good and someone says, Wow! look at that algorithm!"

Teacher: "Little Smitty, can you use the word felonies in a sentence?" Little Smitty: "Yep, yep! I knew a girl that had knees so rough looking, I said she ain't got no lady knees, she got felonies!"

Teacher: "Little Smitty, can you use the word Lamborghini in a sentence?" Little Smitty: "Why yes I can. I knew a person that couldn't tell the difference between animals. So he saw one and asked, Is that a Lamborghini Pig?"

Teacher: "Little Smitty, what comes to mind when you hear about Selma Alabama? Little Smitty: "Well teach, it reminds me of when my daddy had too many vehicles. He had an old truck he didn't drive. He told me "Son, I think Ima Selma truck. Go see if Alabama truck for a good price!"

Teacher: "Little Smitty, can you use the word confederate in a sentence?" Little Smitty: "Well, yeah. The prison guard almost teared up when the confederate some of his food when it looked like the rat was starving!"

Teacher: "Little Smitty, do you know what concrete is?" Little Smitty: "I sure do. It's what prisoners use to pour sidewalks!"

Teacher: "Little Smitty, can you use molasses in a sentence?" Little Smitty: "Ummm yeah. I was in the store when a customer asked. Do y'all sell molasses here? The clerk said, "Hell naw! We don't even sell the moles!"

Teacher: "Little Smitty, what is a jockey?" Little Smitty: "It's what a male athlete uses to start his car or open his house door with!"

Teacher: "Little Smitty, did you hear about the guy that lived on an island who had to take his canoe to cast his vote? Little Smitty: "Yep! And while on the water, he was singing row, row, row your vote."

Teacher: "Little Smitty, can you tell me a genie joke?" Little Smitty: "Sure. There was a man that found a bottle and rubbed it! Lo and behold, a genie appeared and granted him 3 wishes. After the house and the fence, for his third wish, the man asked for a gate. "Poof!" It was done. All of a sudden, another genie appeared and said, "Ok Paul, I see you're out here insta gating again!"

Teacher: (I don't know why she only calls on Little Smitty, but oh well 😂 😂 😂) "Little Smitty, can you use pistachios in a sentence?" Little Smitty: "I don't know why you keep choosing me Teach, but ok, here it goes. My mama bought a junk car from a crooked car lot and now she is pistachios more on the car than what it's worth!"

Teacher: "Little Smitty, can you use the word mildew in a sentence?" Little Smitty: "YEP! When you're hungry, nothing can satisfy you like a good home cooked mildew!"

For a project, the teacher let everyone in the class pick out a wooden letter of the alphabet. They had to say a word and a sentence that started with that letter for class tomorrow. One little girl excitedly said, "Teacher, I got a J!" The teacher said, "That's nice. Put it in your desk for now." A few minutes later Little Smitty shouted out, "Teacher, I gotta P!" The teacher said, "That's nice Little Smitty. Just put it in your desk for now." Little Smitty had to stay after school to clean his desk and mop the floor!

Teacher: "Little Smitty, can you use the word harassment in a sentence?" Little Smitty: "Hell yeah teach. "I dated this girl for three months. But after I caught her cheating, *harassment* nothing to me!"

Teacher: "Little Smitty, can you use the word phobias in a sentence?" Little Smitty: "Why most certainly your teacherness! My lightweight daddy got drunk off of *phobias*. But my mama drank eight and could still stand up straight!"

Teacher: "Little Smitty, can you use Ghana and New Guinea in a sentence?" Little Smitty: "Hell yeah teach! My mama is *Ghana* buy me a *New Guinea* pig cause my other one ran away!"

Teacher: "Little Smitty, can you use the word banana in a sentence?" Little Smitty: "I think I can pull that off teach. I asked my mama could I stay with grandma. She said let me call and run it *banana* first to see if it's ok!"

Teacher: "Little Smitty, can you use the word evaluate in a sentence?" Little Smitty: "Fo sho, fo sho. I saw my friend Valerie pick her nose and put her finger in her mouth. I said *E-Val-u-ate* a booger!"

Teacher: "Little Smitty, can you use the word domain in a sentence?" Little Smitty: "Hecky yeah, teach! We were at my granny's house back in November when my uncle came over and was holding the door open. My daddy told him, "It's cold as hell outside, so please close the damn *do-main*!"

Teacher: "Little Smitty, can you tell me some of the things found in the country Greece?" Little Smitty: "As far as I can remember, my granny always had fried chicken, fried potatoes, hot water cornbread, and fried fish cooked in the country grease!"

Teacher: "Little Smitty, do you know what Ginger Snaps are?" Little Smitty said: "Ginger Snaps because she is tired of Gilligan and that darn deserted island!"

Teacher: "Little Smitty, do you know what a paradox is?" Little Smitty: "Yep! It's two places side by side where you can park two boats or not."

Teacher: "Little Smitty……can you use the word Rigatoni in a sentence?" Little Smitty: "I sure can! Three selection committee officials were fired because they tried to *Rigatoni* Awards show in favor of their less than stellar actor friends!"

Teacher: "Little Smitty, Is Uranus a planet? "Little Smitty: "Nope, but if I drop my pants, it turns into a Moon!"

Teacher: "Little Smitty, where does a stinky person sit in church?" Little Smitty: "Definitely in the "pews!"

Teacher: "Little Smitty, do you know what a mouse pad is?" Little Smitty: "Heck yeah teacher. It's a house or apartment for rodents!"

Teacher: "Little Smitty, can you use the word 'Cancun' in a sentence?" Little Smitty: "Oh yeah. Jed told Granny that he prefers eating fresh raccoon instead of that 'Cancun' she's been cooking lately!"

Teacher: "Little Smitty, can you use the word 'substantiate' in a sentence?" Little Smitty: "It just so happens that I can. When my friend took his girl to the 'substantiate,' three subs 'cause she was pretty hungry!"

Tim "Smitty" Smith

Teacher: Little Smitty, do you know any airplane jokes?" Little Smitty: "Ummmm yeah. An airplane engine manufacturer was testing one of its engines when all of a sudden it broke loose from the stand and started bouncing all over the plant. The sound it was making was Boeing, Boeing, Boeing, Boeing!"

Teacher: "Little Smitty, can you use the word 'September' in a sentence?" Little Smitty: "Why I think I can pull that off. The confused lumberjack screamed everything 'September' when the tree he cut fell down!"

Teacher: "Little Smitty, do you know what a bassinet is? Little Smitty: "I sure do. It's what fishermen put the bass fish that they caught into."

Teacher: "Little Smitty, what can you tell me about Buckingham Palace?" Little Smitty: "Isn't that the place where they have Pig Rodeos?"

Teacher: "Little Smitty, what's the Capitol of Kentucky?" Little Smitty: "K"

Teacher: "Little Smitty, can you finish this sentence, Mary had a little lamb?" Little Smitty: "Accompanied by some mashed potatoes and green beans for dinner and some chocolate cake for dessert! Oh, and a glass of sweet tea!"

Teacher: "Little Smitty, do you know

what a funeral home is? Little Smitty: "A funeral home is just a coroner store!"

Teacher: "Little Smitty, do you know what an Amish Shoe is?" Little Smitty: "Why yeah! It's when someone is longing to see someone they haven't seen in a while, and that's what they say when they finally talk to them!"

Teacher: "Little Smitty, do you know the story of Noah's Ark?" Little Smitty: "Yes, ma'am! Noah had an ark party and invited some people. 'Cain' wasn't 'Abel' to stand up straight so 'Enoch' over some tables. Some people didn't get an invitation. So he will 'Adam' this 'Eve'ning. They had 'Ham' for the party, but the table was crooked. So they had to 'Shem' one of the legs. This party is nice 'Seth' all of the guests! I 'Noah' that's right," 'Cain' agreed. "Because 'Enos' how to throw a party!!

Teacher: "Little Smitty, can you use the word 'fungus' in a sentence?" Little Smitty: "You darn skippy! Anyway, me and my best friend, Gus, don't kick it anymore like we used to. So, the next time I saw him, I told him, "You have changed. You ain't no more 'fun-Gus'!"

In health class, Little Smitty's teacher was explaining to the students the dangers of pills and medicine. She asked the class for a volunteer to explain what should happen if a pill rolls off of a table onto the floor. Little Smitty raised his hand. "Yes, Little Smitty, what should happen?" Little Smitty explained, "Well, at my house, I would call it 'Viagra Falls'!"

Teacher: "Little Smitty, can you use the word 'catastrophe' in a sentence?" Little Smitty: "Sure teach. But you have to say the word slowly to get the full affect. ANYWAY, I went to a cat twerking contest, and the best twerking cat received a 'catastrophe'!"

Teacher: "Little Smitty, can you use the word 'Timbuktu' in a sentence?"

Little Smitty: "Sure. I'll give it a shot. Your Royal Teacherness! My neighbor had a wild horse named Tim. Three cowboys tried to break him. Well, 'Timbuktu' over a fence and the third one into the hog pit!"

Teacher: "Little Smitty, can you say the A,B,C's for me?" Little Smitty: "ABC, ABC, ABC, ABC, ABC!"

Teacher: "Little Smitty, do you know what an astronaut is?" Little Smitty: "Duhhhh! Yeah! It's what George Jetson's dog gets if he runs into a wall headfirst!"

Teacher: "Little Smitty, do you know what cannibals eat?" Little Smitty: "Sure! They eat Mary, Nate, Ted, Chuck Roast!"

Teacher: "Ok, today, class, we are going to learn about your Forefathers!" Little Smitty: "Ummm, teacher, I don't know about the rest of the class. But I only have one daddy!"

Teacher: "Little Smitty, what would you call yellowjackets wearing bras?" Little Smitty: "Ummmmm, BOO BEES?"

Teacher: "Little Smitty, can you use the word 'therapist' in a sentence?" Little Johnny: "Ok, but don't be mad at me. Here it goes. My daddy was mad because he had to give the nurse a urine sample. So after he came out of the bathroom he handed the full cup to the nurse and said, 'THERAPIST'! ARE YOU HAPPY NOW?"

Friendly Jokes

Friend: "Hey Little Smitty, tell me a cannibal joke!" Little Smitty: "I had a good friend that was a cannibal." I said, "Hey dude, let's go grab us some chili dogs for lunch!" He replied, "Ok. But we gotta wait until wintertime. Then we can find one that's tied up outside!"

Rowdy Crowd

Little Smitty was at a rally. I guess it got too rowdy because the police came. All of a sudden a female cop with a bullhorn screamed "DISPERSE! DISPERSE"! All the women got quiet. They looked at the cop that shouted to see what kind of purse she had and what she was going to say about it!

Crazy Things That Happen

Little Smitty ordered a salad with ranch dressing. The waitress brought his salad to the table with a plaid shirt, some rustler jeans, a ten-gallon hat, some cowboy boots, and a lasso.

A neighbor told Little Smitty's dad to rev up his sports car. Little Smitty overheard him, ran in the house, and called his Pastor. He told his Pastor that he needed to come and sit in his daddy's passenger seat for a little while.

Two people met at the same door. They both motioned to each other. One person said, "After you." The other one replied, "No, after you!" This went on a few more times when Little Smitty came up to the door and shouted, "V then W, X, Y, and Z! Now please go through the damn door!"

Little Smitty said, "Mr. Wong loved elevators so much, he rode one from floor to floor for about 3 hours! That's just Wong on so many levels!"

Smitty said, "I once knew a girl named Ella. She loved salmon so much. I called her Salmon Ella! She was poison!"

Little Smitty saw a dog in his yard. He shooed it away. The dog was *ticked* so he *flea'd* the scene.

There was a woman whose clothes were wrinkled. Little Smitty told her that she had an iron deficiency. She was steamed!

Little Smitty sneezed. Alexa instructed him to stay back 6 feet back.

A beaver quit work right in the middle of the day. He really didn't give a *Dam* that day!

While at a doctor's appointment, the physician stated, "Ma'am, you have head lice." She demanded, "Hey, keep your eyes up here mister!"

Little Smitty's Daddy: "Babe, I'm going to the store to get some chicken!"
Little Smitty's Mama: "Okay sweetheart. Grab some breasts while you're there!"
Little Smitty's daddy came home with a knot on his head, two black eyes, and a handprint on the side of his face!

Wild Turkeys
Man at Sandwich shop: "I think I'm going to get a Turkey Club." Little Smitty: "I didn't know turkeys partied like that!"

What The Hell?
Little Smitty went to a friend's house. His friend had Seiko and Timex timepieces attached to 10 parakeets. He asked, "What the hell are you doing?" His friend said, "Birdwatching!"

Wordy Situation
Little Smitty's dog got a hold of his dictionary. The dog ate a few pages. Little Smitty was able to get some of the pages from the dog before he swallowed them. Smitty said, "Bad Dog"! The dog replied, "You took the words right out of my mouth!"

Gone Stamping
Little Smitty went to the post office and asked the worker, "Can I get one stamp, please?" She stomped her left foot and yelled, "Next!"

Funny Food Experiences
Little Smitty witnessed the main chef in a restaurant faint. He yelled, "COOKOUT!"

While at White Castles, Little Smitty ordered 5 Cheeseburgers, fries, and a large Big Red soda. The cashier responded, "Is that to go?" Little Smitty answered, "Yeah, in a few hours. But that's personal!"

Web of Lies
Friend: Did you hear about the man that got caught in a "web" of lies with his girlfriend because he was texting her best friend? Little Smitty: "Yep. She spied her man!"

Rusty Advice

Little Smitty observed Rusty Senior trying to teach his son Rusty Junior how to throw a football. After many attempts, Junior still couldn't grasp the technique. His father said, "Come on, Junior. THROW THE BALL RIGHT!" Little Smitty said, "Hey mister, be patient with him. He's just a little Rusty!"

Smelly Cow

Little Smitty was on a farm looking at some cows when he heard one of them fart. A few seconds later, someone beside him said, "Phew! Where is that smell coming from?" Little Smitty said, "I think it's coming from the dairy air!"

Big Boat, Small Boat

Little Smitty was in a small boat when a much larger boat passed. A chunk of it fell off and landed in his boat. He picked it up. Then shouted, "Piece of ship!"

Miss Polly Has Shingles

Neighbor: "Little Smitty, Miss Polly has got the Shingles!" Little Smitty: "I'm sure she does. But I don't need a new roof!"

Girl Names

Little Smitty knew a girl named Jewel Rhee. She was always worn out!

Little Smitty knew a girl named Penny Nichols. He always knew there was a six cents about her!

Smitty Sayings and Stories

Little Smitty: Undertakers work "enbalmy" conditions!

Little Smitty: "Hey Miss, what do you do for a living?" Lady: "I'm a tutor." Little Smitty: "You might wanna lay off the beans and broccoli then!"

Little Smitty: "Hey man, what do you do for a living?" Man: "I'm a NASCAR driver!" Little Smitty: "That's awesome! My daddy's piece of junk car is not so nice, though!"

Little Smitty was at a baseball game when he heard the umpire shout, "Strike Three!" After he hit the first two people and was going after the third, another fan tackled him and held him down until security came.

Little Smitty was talking to a friend, and after a pause in the conversation, he said, "I'm sleepy!" Just then, six little guys came up to him, punched him in the stomach, and yelled, "YOU AINT OUR BROTHER!!"

Little Smitty was staring at a tree when an older man came up to him and asked why he was fixated on the tree. Little Smitty said, "They said this tree has bark. I just want to hear it one time!"

Little Smitty: "Hey Moses, can you help me across this divided sea?" Moses: "No, I did my part!"

Little Smitty overheard two prunes having a conversation. Prune 1: "What have you been up to?" Prune 2: "Nothing. Just raisin my kids."

Little Smitty dropped his iPhone and liquid started leaking from it! He said, "Ewwww! Apple Juice!"

Neighbor: "Little Smitty, do you know how to get rid of ants?" Little Smitty: "Yep! Call your damn uncles to come and pick them up!"

Little Smitty said, "Did y'all hear about the guy who went to proctology school and couldn't find a job? Well, he found one. Things are really looking up for him!"

Man: "Hey, Little Smitty. What do you call a cop with no money?" Little Smitty: "Po, Po, Po!"

Little Smitty said, "Marijuana doesn't make you faster. But speed does!"

Little Smitty: "I know why everybody calls old people responsible!" Man: "And why is that Little Smitty?" Little Smitty: "Because you can always *Depends* on them!"

Little Smitty saw a rare vehicle, the Yugo, driving past his house. About an hour later, that same vehicle drove past when he yelled, "There Yugo again!"

Little Smitty and his friend, Little Jack were playing outside when all of a sudden, Little Jack had an accident of the number two nature. Little Smitty smelled him and went to tell his mama. "Umm, miss, your son Jack." Jack's mama interrupted him and said, "Don't come in here telling me anything about my son! I know he's not perfect!" "But miss, you don't understand. Ummmm, Jack, ummm." "I said don't tell me nothing about my son. Now go on back and play!" Little Smitty got mad and finally said, "I CAN'T TELL YOU JACK SHIT, CAN I?"

A friend told Little Smitty, "Get ahold of yourself!" Little Smitty shrugged his shoulders, pulled out his cell phone, and then dialed his own number!

Little Smitty went to the DMV. A lady told him he had to get in line. So he replied, "Lady you don't know me. I ALREADY got my life together!"

Friend: "Little Smitty, I got a friend with a lazy eye." Little Smitty: "Well, why doesn't he make it get up and take out the trash or something!"

Little Smitty overheard somebody say, "An eye for an eye and a tooth for a tooth." Little Smitty thought to himself, "They need to be satisfied with their own original parts and stop trading them!"

Little Smitty was in the bathroom when he overheard a urinal and a commode talking. The urinal said, "Man, I STAY pissed!" The commode replied, "I feel ya. I'm constantly going through a lot of shit myself. But I'm not going 'toilet' that stop me up!"

Little Smitty's class took a field trip to a farm. One kid asked the tour guide why the horses were so calm. Little Smitty spoke up, cutting the tour guide off, and said, "Because they live in stable homes!"

Little Smitty whispered to his mother, "Mama, I think Alexa is listening to our conversations!" About 10 seconds later, Alexa lit up and said, "No, I am NOT Little Smitty!"

Little Smitty's friends: "Hey, Little Smitty, tell us a toe joke!" Little Smitty: "OK. A man got his foot caught in a machine. All of his toes got cut off completely! He just knew there was no way he would have toes on that foot again. But he went to the doctor anyway. The doctor tried to convince him that he could re-attach his toes. However, the man was very, very skeptical! Well ,he agreed to the surgery, and when he came to his toes were back on his foot! The doctor walked in, and the man was so happy he said, "Doc, I don't believe you really did it!" The doctor said, "See, I 'toed' ya so!

Friend: "Hey Little Smitty, tell me a skinny girl joke!" Little Smitty: "A skinny girl was late for work. When her boss asked her why, she responded, "I'm sorry. I just got a little behind!"

Little Smitty was in a doctor's office when he overheard an elderly man tell the doctor, "Hey, Doc! Please keep me awake during my colonoscopy so I can watch you-tube!"

Little Smitty had a conversation with a number when it said, "I often feel less than zero!" Little Smitty said, "You sure are a negative one, aren't ya?"

Little Smitty had to have surgery on the top of his right foot at the big toe. Before the surgery, a short, plump prep nurse came in and said she had to "mark" the correct foot and toe for the doctor. She did so with a sharpie. She began to check his other vitals when the doctor came in. He asked him if someone verified the correct toe. Little Smitty told him, "Yes, this little piggy went to mark it!"

Little Smitty was at the beach when all of a sudden, a Seagull landed beside him and started talking to him. The conversation lasted for a few hours, and they became buddies. A lady thought it was peculiar that a human and a bird were having a good time, so she asked Little Smitty who the bird was. Little Smitty replied, "Oh, that's my new gull friend!"

Little Smitty returned something to Walmart. He was trying to be nice by stepping behind the service desk at a register and started pushing buttons. The clerk asked, "What are you doing? You don't work here!" Little Smitty said, "Well, hell, lady, I didn't work here when I checked myself out either!"

Friend: "Little Smitty, what do they call a father that lives in Indiana?" Little Smitty: "Hoosier Daddy!"

Little Smitty saw some cows on a cliff. All of a sudden, he thought, "Well, it looks like the steaks are pretty high!"

Friend: "Hey, Little Smitty, what does a tiger say when he wants his story to be believable?" Little Smitty replied, "I ain't Lion?"

Little Smitty overheard a woman say to her very drunk, heavy friend on the floor when she tried to pick her up, I CAN'T STAND YOU!"

Little Smitty said a woman got caught stealing at Victoria's Secret. She took some panties and some bras. He said she went to jail and enrolled in school. She landed a job as an Undie Taker."

Little Smitty saw a man soaking wet and smelling like alcohol coming out of a bar! He asked him, "What happened to you, sir?" The man said, "I don't know Little Smitty. Everything was going great until I told everyone, ALL DRINKS ON ME!"

Little Smitty went to church and afterward asked the pastor what his name was. The pastor said, "Howard be thy name!"

Friend: "Little Smitty, since you know everything, what is Darth Vader's sister's name? Little Smitty: "Ella. She has her ups and downs. Everybody pushes her buttons. But she welcomes everybody to ride her!"

Little Smitty was asked which man a woman would call a dog. A man that had been drinking or a man that had not been drinking. Little Smitty said, "Definitely the man that had not been drinking because I saw the sober man pinch her!"

Little Smitty was at a wedding when the preacher said that the couple has written their own vows. The wife went first, and as she started to read what she had written, Little Smitty stood up and screamed, COME ON LADY! JUST SAY A-E-I-O-U! AND SOMETIMES Y, I DO, AND LET'S GO CUT THAT CAKE!"

Little Smitty was walking beside a church, and he heard a conversation through an open window about the Sopranos of the choir not liking the baritones and bass choir members. Little Smitty peeked in the window and said, "Awww, y'all are just "low key hating!"

Little Smitty saw a frog that was doing backflips and giggling after each flip. He went over to the frog and asked him what the hell was wrong with him. The frog said, "Nothing! I'm just having A Reptile Dysfunction!"

Little Smitty saw that Piglet was feeling left out by Pooh because they hadn't hung out in a while. Pooh asked him what he could do to make things better. Piglet replied, "Just Bear with me for a little while!"

Little Smitty to a man raking leaves: "Hey, mister, what are sycamore trees? Man raking leaves: "I'm really 'sycamore trees' from my neighbor's yards dropping their leaves in my yard!"

A grandfather clock factory closed down. Little Smitty asked the owner what happened with his lease. The owner explained, "We just ran out of time!"

Little Smitty had a cold and sneezed so hard that green stuff from his nose was all over his face. Some people around him started laughing at him. Little Smitty yelled, "Hey, it's 'snot' funny!"

A neighbor asked Little Smitty why his grass was wet early in the morning, and it hadn't rained. Little Smitty said that it had dew on it! The neighbor then answered, "Oh no! Just make sure you don't step in it. Damn dogs!"

Little Smitty went to the store with his dad when his mom called. "Get some ribs." Little Smitty told her, "Ok. I'll tell Dad to 'Adam' to the list!"

Little Smitty went to the gas station with his father to get some gas. His father lifted the nozzle, ready to pump, when the cashier spoke over the speaker system, "Sir, that pump is prepaid!" Little Smitty shouted, "Cool! Hey Dad, we need to find the person that paid for our gas so we can thank them!"

Little Smitty saw two prisoners on their way to the guillotine. He ran up to them and asked, "So where will y'all be headed today?"

Friend: "Little Smitty, tell me a guillotine joke!" Little Smitty: "A chatty guillotine operator will talk your head off!"

Little Smitty was walking in the woods when he observed two beavers building a dam. All of a sudden, a hungry owl swooped down to capture one of the beavers but missed and got stuck in the dam. Little Smitty, speaking with astonishment, screeched, "Well, Owl Be Damned!"

Little Smitty was at church one Sunday when the pastor exclaimed, "Tell your neighbor that you love them!" Little Smitty stood up and refuted, "Sorry, pastor! I am not driving all the way back home right now. I'll tell them after church!"

Little Smitty was walking when he met a large man carrying a hurt donkey on his back. Little Smitty inquired, "Hey mister, wanna hear a joke?" The man responded, "Sure!" Little Smitty told him the joke, and the man laughed uncontrollably that he dropped his donkey! Yep! He actually laughed his ass off!

Friend: "Little Smitty, what do you call a 'Lady of the night' who finished Law School? Little Smitty: "A Prostituting Attorney!"

Little Smitty: "Did y'all know that Eve had the very first McRib sandwich? It was from 'McGardens.' I 'Noah' that for a fact!"

Little Smitty was sitting in the woods listening to the trees sing and whistle

with the wind. He was bobbing his head to the tree music. A hiker walked up to him. "What are you listening to that seems to be so good?"
Little Smitty: "Knotty By Nature!"

Little Smitty went on a trip through Carnival vacations. The captain put the ship on 'Cruise' control.

An Idaho potato and a sweet potato were in a restaurant kitchen. A new chef couldn't tell the difference between them. He talked to both potatoes, "Which one of y'all is the Sweet Potato?" The sweet potato spoke up, "I yam!"

Little Smitty's granny is so old that she smoked some dinosaur ribs for Thanksgiving. Somebody jokingly inquired, "Well did they at least smell good?" Little Smitty shouted, "Hell naw! 'Extinct'!"

Mr. Cain is supported by his family members – Lana, Cole, Harry, Candy, and Walken. Lana is just itching for attention. Cole is nosy. Harry is in and out like the wind. Candy is so sweet. Walken is always lending support.

Little Smitty went to a department store and saw a non-human male figure modeling clothes. He yelled, "Mannequin!" Then he walked over to the women's department and saw the female version. He shouted, "Womannequin!"

Little Smitty went to McDonalds and ordered a Quarter Pounder. The dumb cashier went to the back and brought him back a hammer and a .25-cent piece. Then instructed, "Watch your fingers when you hit the coin!"

Little Smitty says: "Yo daddy is soooooo stupid, the car dealership told him he needed to get his tires rotated. Then yo stupid daddy told them, "No, I don't. They rotate every time I drive my car!"

Little Smitty's daddy told him that his mother always trips over her words and pronounces many words wrong. Little Smitty tried to comfort his daddy by saying, "Poor Grammar."

Little Smitty was exhausted as the last cow was rounded up after a fence broke. There was one smart-ass cow in the bunch who vowed to Little Smitty, "The next time, you won't catch me!" Little Smitty: "What did you say?" The smart-ass cow roared back, "You herd me!"

Little Smitty went deep sea diving during Christmas. He was disappointed because he did not get to see any big fish. He said, "No whale, no whale!"

Little Smitty was in a store when he saw some cereal that said '33% More Free' on the box. Little Smitty poured out 1/3 of the cereal into a bag and walked out of the store.

Friend: "Little Smitty, how do you feel?"
Little Smitty: "Mostly with my hands!"

The Woman of the Garden of Eden asked the man what was December 24th? The man hollered, "It's Christmas Eve!"

Friend: "Hey, Little Smitty, what is one thing a proctologist should never say if the patient passes out and then wakes up with terrible vision?" Little Smitty: "How many fingers do I have up?"

Little Smitty went to a restaurant to eat. The food was so good, he decided to go back to the kitchen. One of the workers stopped him and inquired, "I'm sorry, sir, but what are you doing back here?" Little Smitty; "My food was soooo good, that I could tell it was homemade. I just wanted to see which 'hoe made' it!"

Friend: "Little Smitty, why do you always say yes to everything? "Little Smitty: "I just don't no!"

Little Smitty: "Why can't a leopard ever get away if he escapes?" Friend: "I don't know. Why?" Little Smitty:"Because he is always spotted wherever he goes!"

Little Smitty says: "If your last name is Utt, please don't name your daughter Edie!"

Little Smitty accidentally swallowed some alphabet letters he had in his mouth. His mother called the doctor and asked him what should she do! The doctor calmly told her, "Just be patient and wait for him to have a Vowel Movement!"

"If a prostitute robs you, is that called a 'Hoe'd' Up?"

Neighbor: "Little Smitty, I saw dew on your grass this morning." Little Smitty: "I'm gonna kill that dog across the street!"

Neighbor: "Little Smitty, can you tell me a granny joke?" Little Smitty: "Yo little granny is soooooooooo stupid. I saw her screaming at a blouse the other day, GET OUT OF THERE! GET OUT OF THERE NOW!" I asked her what she was doing. This dummy told me, "The television commercial assured me that to get rid of a tough stain, I needed to shout it out!"

Little Smitty: "Mr. and Mrs. Potato Head had 3 kids. They were Tater Tots!"

If you ask how they are doing, they will say, "We, are *Ore-Ida*!"

A man with a toupee was going outside from a building while it was sleeting pretty badly. Little Smitty: "Mister, I wouldn't go out there right now because you'll have hail toupee!"